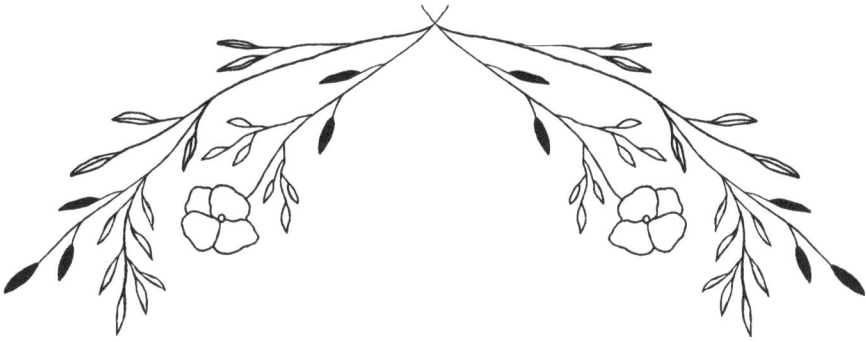

Prayer Journal for Women:
90 Days of
Praise, Prayer & Gratitude
through the Psalms

This Journal Belongs To:

_____

O come, let us sing
unto the Lord
Let us make a joyful noise to
the rock of our salvation.

Psalm 95:1

I will be glad and rejoice in you.
I will sing praise to your name, O Most High.
Psalm 9:2

Lord, today I will praise you for...

_____

_____

_____

_____

Consider my affliction and my travail.
Forgive all my sins. Psalm 25:18

Lord, I confess...

_____

_____

_____

_____

For his loving kindness is great toward us.
The Lord's faithfulness endures forever. Psalm 117:2

Today, Lord I am grateful for...

_____

_____

_____

_____

_____

_____

What profit is there in my destruction,
if I go down to the pit? Shall the dust praise you?
Shall it declare your truth? Psalm 30:9

Prayers

_____

_____

_____

_____

_____

_____

_____

_____

_____

_____

_____

_____

_____

_____

_____

Answered Prayers

_____

_____

_____

_____

My tongue shall talk about your righteousness and about your praise all day long. Psalm 35:28

Lord, today I will praise you for...

_____

_____

_____

_____

Deliver us, and forgive our sins, for your name's sake. Psalm 79:9

Lord, I confess...

_____

_____

_____

_____

I will praise the name of God with a song, and will magnify him with thanksgiving. Psalm 69:30

Today, Lord I am grateful for...

_____

_____

_____

_____

_____

_____

Hear my prayer, O Lord!
Let my cry come to you. Psalm 102:1

Prayers

_____

_____

_____

_____

_____

_____

_____

_____

_____

_____

_____

_____

_____

_____

_____

_____

Answered Prayers

_____

_____

_____

Sing praises to God! Sing praises!
Sing praises to our King! Sing praises!
Psalm 47:6

Lord, today I will praise you for...

_____

_____

_____

_____

O Lord, have mercy on me! Heal me,
for I have sinned against you." Psalm 41:4

Lord, I confess...

_____

_____

_____

_____

So we, your people and sheep of your pasture, will give you thanks
forever. We will praise you forever, to all generations. Psalm 79:13

Today, Lord I am grateful for...

_____

_____

_____

_____

_____

_____

Hear the voice of my petitions,
when I cry to you, when I lift up my hands
toward your Most Holy Place. Psalm 28:2

Prayers

_____

_____

_____

_____

_____

_____

_____

_____

_____

_____

_____

_____

_____

_____

Answered Prayers

_____

_____

_____

Lord, open my lips.
My mouth will declare your praise.
Psalm 51:15

Lord, today I will praise you for... _____

_____

_____

_____

Deliver us, and forgive our sins, for your name's sake.
Psalm 79:9b

Lord, I confess... _____

_____

_____

_____

Let's come before his presence with thanksgiving.
Let's extol him with songs! Psalm 95:2

Today, Lord I am grateful for... _____

_____

_____

_____

_____

_____

Hear, O Lord, my prayer.
Listen to the voice of my petitions.
Psalm 86:6

Prayers

_____

_____

_____

_____

_____

_____

_____

_____

_____

_____

_____

_____

_____

_____

_____

_____

_____

Answered Prayers

_____

_____

_____

_____

My heart is steadfast, God. My heart is steadfast.
I will sing, yes, I will sing praises.
Psalm 57:7

Lord, today I will praise you for...

_____

_____

_____

_____

Sins overwhelmed me,
but you atoned for our transgressions. Psalms 65:3

Lord, I confess...

_____

_____

_____

_____

Let them offer the sacrifices of thanksgiving,
and declare his deeds with singing Psalm 107:22

Today, Lord I am grateful for...

_____

_____

_____

_____

_____

_____

Lord, hear my voice. Let your ears be attentive to the voice of my petitions. Psalm 130:2

Prayers

_____
_____
_____
_____
_____
_____
_____
_____
_____
_____
_____
_____
_____
_____

Answered Prayers

_____
_____
_____

Date _____

*Praise be to the Lord God,
the God of Israel, who alone does marvelous deeds.
Psalm 72:18*

Lord, today I will praise you for...

_____
_____
_____
_____

*Create in me a clean heart, O God.
Renew a right spirit within me. Psalm 51:10*

Lord, I confess...

_____
_____
_____
_____

*I will give thanks to the Lord
according to his righteousness, Psalm 7:17*

Today, Lord I am grateful for...

_____
_____
_____
_____
_____
_____

Hear my prayer, O Lord. Listen to my petitions
In your faithfulness and righteousness, relieve me.
Psalm 143:1

Prayers

_____

_____

_____

_____

_____

_____

_____

_____

_____

_____

_____

_____

_____

_____

Answered Prayers

_____

_____

_____

To you, my strength, I will sing praises.
For God is my high tower, the God of my mercy.
Psalm 59:17

Lord, today I will praise you for... _____

_____

_____

_____

_____

Wash me thoroughly from my iniquity.
Cleanse me from my sin. Psalm 51:2

Lord, I confess... _____

_____

_____

_____

Sing praise to the Lord, you saints of his.
Give thanks to his holy name. Psalm 30:4

Today, Lord I am grateful for... _____

_____

_____

_____

_____

_____

Let my soul live, that I may praise you.
Let your ordinances help me. Psalm 119:175

Prayers
_____
_____
_____
_____
_____
_____
_____
_____
_____
_____
_____
_____
_____
_____
_____
_____
_____

Answered Prayers
_____
_____
_____
_____

Date _____

*Because your loving kindness is better than life,
my lips shall praise you Psalm 63:3*

Lord, today I will praise you for...

_____
_____
_____
_____

*Hide your face from my sins,
and blot out all of my iniquities. Psalm 51:9*

Lord, I confess...

_____
_____
_____
_____

*I will give thanks to you, Lord, among the peoples.
I will sing praises to you among the nations. Psalm 57:9*

Today, Lord I am grateful for...

_____
_____
_____
_____
_____
_____

Listen to my prayer, God.
Don't hide yourself from my supplication.
Psalm 55:1

Prayers

_____

_____

_____

_____

_____

_____

_____

_____

_____

_____

_____

_____

_____

_____

Answered Prayers

_____

_____

_____

Date _____

Let the peoples praise you, God.
Let all the peoples praise you. Psalm 67:5

Lord, today I will praise you for...

_____
_____
_____
_____

You have set our iniquities before you,
our secret sins in the light of your presence. Psalm 90:8

Lord, I confess...

_____
_____
_____
_____

We give thanks to you, God. We give thanks,
for your Name is near. Psalm 75:1a

Today, Lord I am grateful for...

_____
_____
_____
_____
_____
_____

Answer me when I call, God of my righteousness.
Give me relief from my distress. Have mercy on me,
and hear my prayer. Psalm 4:1

Prayers

_____

_____

_____

_____

_____

_____

_____

_____

_____

_____

_____

_____

_____

_____

_____

Answered Prayers

_____

_____

_____

I will praise the name of God with a song,
and will magnify him with thanksgiving.
Psalm 69:30

Lord, today I will praise you for...

_____

_____

_____

_____

Deliver us, and forgive our sins, for your name's sake.
Psalm 79:9b

Lord, I confess...

_____

_____

_____

_____

Sing praise to Yahweh, you saints of his.
Give thanks to his holy name. Psalm 30:4

Today, Lord I am grateful for...

_____

_____

_____

_____

_____

_____

Let my soul live, that I may praise you.
Let your ordinances help me. Psalm 119:175

Prayers

_____

_____

_____

_____

_____

_____

_____

_____

_____

_____

_____

_____

_____

_____

_____

_____

Answered Prayers

_____

_____

_____

_____

My lips shall shout for joy!
My soul, which you have redeemed, sings praises to you!
Psalm 71:23

Lord, today I will praise you for...

_____

_____

_____

_____

O Lord, have mercy on me! Heal me,
for I have sinned against you." Psalm 41:4

Lord, I confess...

_____

_____

_____

_____

I will give thanks to you, Lord, among the peoples.
I will sing praises to you among the nations. Psalm 57:9

Today, Lord I am grateful for...

_____

_____

_____

_____

_____

_____

Hear my prayer, O Lord, and give ear to my cry.
Don't be silent at my tears. Psalm 39:12a

Prayers

_____

_____

_____

_____

_____

_____

_____

_____

_____

_____

_____

_____

_____

_____

Answered Prayers

_____

_____

_____

I will praise you, Lord my God, with my whole heart.
I will glorify your name forever more. Psalm 86:12

Lord, today I will praise you for...

_____

_____

_____

_____

God, you know my foolishness.
My sins aren't hidden from you. Psalm 69:5

Lord, I confess...

_____

_____

_____

_____

We give thanks to you, God. We give thanks, for your
Name is near. Men tell about your wondrous works.
Psalm 75:1

Today, Lord I am grateful for...

_____

_____

_____

_____

_____

_____

Listen to my prayer, God.
Don't hide yourself from my supplication. Psalm 55:1

Prayers

_____

_____

_____

_____

_____

_____

_____

_____

_____

_____

_____

_____

_____

_____

_____

Answered Prayers

_____

_____

_____

Make a joyful noise to the Lord, all the earth!
Burst out and sing for joy, yes, sing praises!
Psalm 98:4

Lord, today I will praise you for... _____

_____

_____

_____

You have set our iniquities before you,
our secret sins in the light of your presence. Psalm 90:8

Lord, I confess... _____

_____

_____

_____

Give thanks to the Lord! Call on his name!
Make his doings known among the peoples. Psalm 105:1

Today, Lord I am grateful for... _____

_____

_____

_____

_____

_____

Answer me when I call, God of my righteousness.
Give me relief from my distress. Have mercy on me,
and hear my prayer. Psalm 4:1

Prayers

_____

_____

_____

_____

_____

_____

_____

_____

_____

_____

_____

_____

_____

_____

Answered Prayers

_____

_____

_____

_____

For the Lord is great, and greatly to be praised!
He is to be feared above all gods. Psalm 96:4

Lord, today I will praise you for...

_____

_____

_____

_____

Hide your face from my sins,
and blot out all of my iniquities. Psalm 51:9

Lord, I confess...

_____

_____

_____

_____

Praise the Lord! Give thanks to the Lord, for he is good,
for his loving kindness endures forever. Psalm 106:1

Today, Lord I am grateful for...

_____

_____

_____

_____

_____

_____

Hear, O Lord, my righteous plea.
Give ear to my prayer that doesn't go out of deceitful lips.
Psalm 17:1

Prayers

_____

_____

_____

_____

_____

_____

_____

_____

_____

_____

_____

_____

_____

_____

_____

_____

Answered Prayers

_____

_____

_____

_____

I will sing of loving kindness and justice.
To you, O Lord, I will sing praises. Psalm 101:1

Lord, today I will praise you for...

_____

_____

_____

_____

Wash me thoroughly from my iniquity.
Cleanse me from my sin. Psalm 51:2

Lord, I confess...

_____

_____

_____

_____

I will give great thanks to the Lord with my mouth.
Yes, I will praise him among the multitude. Psalm 109:30

Today, Lord I am grateful for...

_____

_____

_____

_____

_____

_____

Hear my prayer, God.
Listen to the words of my mouth. Psalm 54:2

Prayers

_____

_____

_____

_____

_____

_____

_____

_____

_____

_____

_____

_____

_____

_____

_____

Answered Prayers

_____

_____

_____

Praise the Lord, my soul!
All that is within me, praise his holy name!
Psalm 103:1

Lord, today I will praise you for...

_____

_____

_____

_____

Create in me a clean heart, O God.
Renew a right spirit within me. Psalm 51:10

Lord, I confess...

_____

_____

_____

_____

Give thanks to the Lord, for he is good,
for his loving kindness endures forever. Psalm 118:1

Today, Lord I am grateful for...

_____

_____

_____

_____

_____

Blessed be God, who has not turned away my prayer,
nor his loving kindness from me. Psalm 66:20

Prayers

_____

_____

_____

_____

_____

_____

_____

_____

_____

_____

_____

_____

_____

_____

_____

_____

Answered Prayers

_____

_____

_____

_____

Date _____

Praise the Lord, my soul,
and don't forget all his benefits. Psalm 103:2

Lord, today I will praise you for...

_____

_____

_____

_____

Sins overwhelmed me,
but you atoned for our transgressions. Psalms 65:3

Lord, I confess...

_____

_____

_____

_____

I will give thanks to you, for you have answered me,
and have become my salvation. Psalm 118:21

Today, Lord I am grateful for...

_____

_____

_____

_____

_____

_____

Let my prayer enter into your presence.
Turn your ear to my cry. Psalm 88:2

Prayers

_____

_____

_____

_____

_____

_____

_____

_____

_____

_____

_____

_____

_____

_____

_____

Answered Prayers

_____

_____

_____

I will sing to the Lord as long as I live.
I will sing praise to my God while I have any being.
Psalm 104:33

Lord, today I will praise you for...

_____

_____

_____

_____

Consider my affliction and my travail.
Forgive all my sins. Psalm 25:18

Lord, I confess...

_____

_____

_____

_____

You are my God, and I will give thanks to you.
You are my God, I will exalt you. Psalm 118:28

Today, Lord I am grateful for...

_____

_____

_____

_____

_____

_____

Hear, O Lord, and answer me,
for I am poor and needy. Psalm 86:1

Prayers

_____

_____

_____

_____

_____

_____

_____

_____

_____

_____

_____

_____

_____

_____

_____

Answered Prayers

_____

_____

_____

Sing to him, sing praises to him!
Tell of all his marvelous works.
Psalm 105:2

Lord, today I will praise you for...

_____

_____

_____

_____

You have set our iniquities before you,
our secret sins in the light of your presence. Psalm 90:8

Lord, I confess...

_____

_____

_____

_____

Oh give thanks to the God of heaven;
for his loving kindness endures forever. Psalm 136:26

Today, Lord I am grateful for...

_____

_____

_____

_____

_____

_____

But to you, Yahweh, I have cried.
In the morning, my prayer comes before you.
Psalm 88:13

Prayers

_____

_____

_____

_____

_____

_____

_____

_____

_____

_____

_____

_____

_____

_____

_____

_____

Answered Prayers

_____

_____

_____

Date _____

*Praise the Lord! Give thanks to the Lord,
for he is good, for his loving kindness endures forever.
Psalm 106:1*

Lord, today I will praise you for...

_____
_____
_____
_____

*Hide your face from my sins,
and blot out all of my iniquities. Psalm 51:9*

Lord, I confess...

_____
_____
_____
_____

*Let's come before his presence with thanksgiving.
Let's extol him with songs! Psalm 95:2*

Today, Lord I am grateful for...

_____
_____
_____
_____
_____
_____

Hear my prayer, O Lord!
Let my cry come to you. Psalm 102:1

Prayers

_____

_____

_____

_____

_____

_____

_____

_____

_____

_____

_____

_____

_____

_____

_____

_____

Answered Prayers

_____

_____

_____

_____

From the rising of the sun to its going down,
the Lord's name is to be praised. Psalm 113:3

Lord, today I will praise you for...

_____

_____

_____

_____

Deliver us, and forgive our sins, for your name's sake.
Psalm 79:9b

Lord, I confess...

_____

_____

_____

_____

Let them offer the sacrifices of thanksgiving,
and declare his deeds with singing Psalm 107:22

Today, Lord I am grateful for...

_____

_____

_____

_____

_____

Lord, hear my voice. Let your ears be attentive to the voice of my petitions. Psalm 130:2

Prayers
_____
_____
_____
_____
_____
_____
_____
_____
_____
_____
_____
_____
_____
_____
_____
_____
_____

Answered Prayers
_____
_____
_____
_____

But we will bless the Lord,
from this time forward and forever more.
Praise the Lord! Psalm 115:18

Lord, today I will praise you for...

_____

_____

_____

_____

Sins overwhelmed me,
but you atoned for our transgressions. Psalms 65:3

Lord, I confess...

_____

_____

_____

_____

I will give thanks to you, Lord, among the peoples.
I will sing praises to you among the nations. Psalm 57:9

Today, Lord I am grateful for...

_____

_____

_____

_____

_____

_____

Hear my prayer, O Lord, and give ear to my cry.
Don't be silent at my tears. Psalm 39:12a

Prayers

_____

_____

_____

_____

_____

_____

_____

_____

_____

_____

_____

_____

_____

_____

Answered Prayers

_____

_____

_____

_____

Let my lips utter praise,
for you teach me your statutes. Psalm 119:171

Lord, today I will praise you for...

_____

_____

_____

_____

Wash me thoroughly from my iniquity.
Cleanse me from my sin. Psalm 51:2

Lord, I confess...

_____

_____

_____

_____

Praise the Lord! Give thanks to the Lord, for he is good,
for his loving kindness endures forever. Psalm 106:1

Today, Lord I am grateful for...

_____

_____

_____

_____

_____

_____

Listen to my prayer, God.
Don't hide yourself from my supplication. Psalm 55:1

Prayers

_____

_____

_____

_____

_____

_____

_____

_____

_____

_____

_____

_____

_____

_____

_____

_____

_____

Answered Prayers

_____

_____

_____

I will exalt you, my God, the King.
I will praise your name forever and ever.
Psalm 145:1

Lord, today I will praise you for...

_____

_____

_____

_____

Create in me a clean heart, O God.
Renew a right spirit within me. Psalm 51:10

Lord, I confess...

_____

_____

_____

_____

Give thanks to the Lord! Call on his name!
Make his doings known among the peoples. Psalm 105:1

Today, Lord I am grateful for...

_____

_____

_____

_____

_____

_____

Blessed be God, who has not turned away my prayer,
nor his loving kindness from me. Psalm 66:20

Prayers

_____

_____

_____

_____

_____

_____

_____

_____

_____

_____

_____

_____

_____

_____

_____

_____

Answered Prayers

_____

_____

_____

Every day I will praise you.
I will extol your name forever and ever. Psalm 145:2

Lord, today I will praise you for...

_____

_____

_____

_____

Deliver us, and forgive our sins, for your name's sake.
Psalm 79:9b

Lord, I confess...

_____

_____

_____

_____

Enter into his gates with thanksgiving, and into his courts with praise.
Give thanks to him, and bless his name. Psalm 100:4

Today, Lord I am grateful for...

_____

_____

_____

_____

_____

_____

Hear my prayer, O Lord. Listen to my petitions.
In your faithfulness and righteousness, relieve me.
Psalm 143:1

Prayers

_____

_____

_____

_____

_____

_____

_____

_____

_____

_____

_____

_____

_____

_____

_____

Answered Prayers

_____

_____

_____

_____

While I live, I will praise the Lord.
I will sing praises to my God as long as I exist.
Psalm 146:2

Lord, today I will praise you for...

_____

_____

_____

_____

O Lord, have mercy on me! Heal me,
for I have sinned against you." Psalm 41:4

Lord, I confess...

_____

_____

_____

_____

Sing praise to the Lord, you saints of his.
Give thanks to his holy name. Psalm 30:4

Today, Lord I am grateful for...

_____

_____

_____

_____

_____

_____

Hear my prayer, O God.
Listen to the words of my mouth.
Psalm 54:2

Prayers
_____
_____
_____
_____
_____
_____
_____
_____
_____
_____
_____
_____
_____

Answered Prayers
_____
_____
_____

Praise the Lord, for it is good to sing praises to our God;
for it is pleasant and fitting to praise him. Psalm 147:1

Lord, today I will praise you for...

_____

_____

_____

_____

God, you know my foolishness.
My sins aren't hidden from you. Psalm 69:5

Lord, I confess...

_____

_____

_____

_____

Give thanks to the Lord, for he is good,
for his loving kindness endures forever. Psalm 118:1

Today, Lord I am grateful for...

_____

_____

_____

_____

_____

_____

Hear the voice of my petitions, when I cry to you,
when I lift up my hands toward your
Most Holy Place. Psalm 28:2

Prayers

_____

_____

_____

_____

_____

_____

_____

_____

_____

_____

_____

_____

_____

_____

_____

Answered Prayers

_____

_____

_____

_____

Let everything that has breath praise the Lord!
Praise the Lord!
Psalm 150:6

Lord, today I will praise you for...

_____

_____

_____

_____

Consider my affliction and my travail.
Forgive all my sins. Psalm 25:18

Lord, I confess...

_____

_____

_____

_____

You are my God, and I will give thanks to you.
You are my God, I will exalt you. Psalm 118:28

Today, Lord I am grateful for...

_____

_____

_____

_____

_____

_____

Let my prayer enter into your presence.
Turn your ear to my cry.
Psalm 88:2

Prayers

_____

_____

_____

_____

_____

_____

_____

_____

_____

_____

_____

_____

_____

_____

_____

_____

Answered Prayers

_____

_____

_____

_____

O come, let us sing unto the Lord
Let us make a joyful noise to the rock of our salvation.
Psalm 95:1

Lord, today I will praise you for...

_____

_____

_____

O Lord, have mercy on me! Heal me,
for I have sinned against you." Psalm 41:4

Lord, I confess...

_____

_____

_____

Oh give thanks to the God of heaven;
for his loving kindness endures forever. Psalm 136:26

Today, Lord I am grateful for...

_____

_____

_____

_____

_____

Hear, O Lord, my righteous plea.
Give ear to my prayer that doesn't go out of deceitful lips.
Psalm 17:1

Prayers

_____

_____

_____

_____

_____

_____

_____

_____

_____

_____

_____

_____

_____

_____

_____

_____

Answered Prayers

_____

_____

_____

_____

My mouth will speak the praise of the Lord.
Let all flesh bless his holy name forever and ever.
Psalm 145:21

Lord, today I will praise you for...

_____

_____

_____

_____

Hide your face from my sins,
and blot out all of my iniquities. Psalm 51:9

Lord, I confess...

_____

_____

_____

_____

I will praise the name of God with a song,
and will magnify him with thanksgiving. Psalm 69:30

Today, Lord I am grateful for...

_____

_____

_____

_____

_____

But to you, Yahweh, I have cried.
In the morning, my prayer comes before you.
Psalm 88:13

Prayers
_____
_____
_____
_____
_____
_____
_____
_____
_____
_____
_____
_____
_____
_____

Answered Prayers
_____
_____
_____
_____

But we will bless the Lord,
From this time
forward and forever more.
Praise the Lord!

Psalm 115:18

My lips shall shout for joy!
My soul, which you have redeemed, sings praises to you!
Psalm 71:23

Lord, today I will praise you for...

_____

_____

_____

_____

O Lord, have mercy on me! Heal me,
for I have sinned against you." Psalm 41:4

Lord, I confess...

_____

_____

_____

_____

I will give thanks to you, Lord, among the peoples.
I will sing praises to you among the nations. Psalm 57:9

Today, Lord I am grateful for...

_____

_____

_____

_____

_____

_____

Hear my prayer, O Lord, and give ear to my cry.
Don't be silent at my tears. Psalm 39:12a

Prayers

_____

_____

_____

_____

_____

_____

_____

_____

_____

_____

_____

_____

_____

_____

Answered Prayers

_____

_____

_____

_____

Date _____

I will praise you, Lord my God, with my whole heart.
I will glorify your name forever more. Psalm 86:12

Lord, today I will praise you for...

_____

_____

_____

_____

God, you know my foolishness.
My sins aren't hidden from you. Psalm 69:5

Lord, I confess...

_____

_____

_____

_____

We give thanks to you, God. We give thanks, for your
Name is near. Men tell about your wondrous works.
Psalm 75:1

Today, Lord I am grateful for...

_____

_____

_____

_____

_____

_____

Listen to my prayer, God.
Don't hide yourself from my supplication. Psalm 55:1

Prayers

_____

_____

_____

_____

_____

_____

_____

_____

_____

_____

_____

_____

_____

_____

_____

Answered Prayers

_____

_____

_____

Make a joyful noise to the Lord, all the earth!
Burst out and sing for joy, yes, sing praises!
Psalm 98:4

Lord, today I will praise you for...

_____

_____

_____

_____

You have set our iniquities before you,
our secret sins in the light of your presence. Psalm 90:8

Lord, I confess...

_____

_____

_____

_____

Give thanks to the Lord! Call on his name!
Make his doings known among the peoples. Psalm 105:1

Today, Lord I am grateful for...

_____

_____

_____

_____

_____

_____

Answer me when I call, God of my righteousness.
Give me relief from my distress. Have mercy on me,
and hear my prayer. Psalm 4:1

Prayers

_____

_____

_____

_____

_____

_____

_____

_____

_____

_____

_____

_____

_____

_____

Answered Prayers

_____

_____

_____

For the Lord is great, and greatly to be praised!
He is to be feared above all gods. Psalm 96:4

Lord, today I will praise you for...

_____

_____

_____

_____

Hide your face from my sins,
and blot out all of my iniquities. Psalm 51:9

Lord, I confess...

_____

_____

_____

_____

Praise the Lord! Give thanks to the Lord, for he is good,
for his loving kindness endures forever. Psalm 106:1

Today, Lord I am grateful for...

_____

_____

_____

_____

_____

_____

Hear, O Lord, my righteous plea.
Give ear to my prayer that doesn't go out of deceitful lips.
Psalm 17:1

Prayers

_____

_____

_____

_____

_____

_____

_____

_____

_____

_____

_____

_____

_____

_____

_____

Answered Prayers

_____

_____

_____

I will sing of loving kindness and justice.
To you, O Lord, I will sing praises. Psalm 101:1

Lord, today I will praise you for...

_____

_____

_____

_____

Wash me thoroughly from my iniquity.
Cleanse me from my sin. Psalm 51:2

Lord, I confess...

_____

_____

_____

_____

I will give great thanks to the Lord with my mouth.
Yes, I will praise him among the multitude. Psalm 109:30

Today, Lord I am grateful for...

_____

_____

_____

_____

_____

_____

Hear my prayer, God.
Listen to the words of my mouth. Psalm 54:2

Prayers
_____
_____
_____
_____
_____
_____
_____
_____
_____
_____
_____
_____
_____
_____
_____

Answered Prayers
_____
_____
_____
_____

Date _____

Praise the Lord, my soul!
All that is within me, praise his holy name!
Psalm 103:1

Lord, today I will praise you for...

_____

_____

_____

_____

Create in me a clean heart, O God.
Renew a right spirit within me. Psalm 51:10

Lord, I confess...

_____

_____

_____

_____

Give thanks to the Lord, for he is good,
for his loving kindness endures forever. Psalm 118:1

Today, Lord I am grateful for...

_____

_____

_____

_____

_____

_____

Blessed be God, who has not turned away my prayer,
nor his loving kindness from me. Psalm 66:20

Prayers

_____

_____

_____

_____

_____

_____

_____

_____

_____

_____

_____

_____

_____

_____

Answered Prayers

_____

_____

_____

Praise the Lord, my soul,
and don't forget all his benefits. Psalm 103:2

Lord, today I will praise you for...

_____

_____

_____

_____

Sins overwhelmed me,
but you atoned for our transgressions. Psalms 65:3

Lord, I confess...

_____

_____

_____

_____

I will give thanks to you, for you have answered me,
and have become my salvation. Psalm 118:21

Today, Lord I am grateful for...

_____

_____

_____

_____

_____

_____

Let my prayer enter into your presence.
Turn your ear to my cry. Psalm 88:2

Prayers

_____

_____

_____

_____

_____

_____

_____

_____

_____

_____

_____

_____

_____

_____

_____

Answered Prayers

_____

_____

_____

I will sing to the Lord as long as I live.
I will sing praise to my God while I have any being.
Psalm 104:33

Lord, today I will praise you for...

_____

_____

_____

_____

Consider my affliction and my travail.
Forgive all my sins. Psalm 25:18

Lord, I confess...

_____

_____

_____

_____

You are my God, and I will give thanks to you.
You are my God, I will exalt you. Psalm 118:28

Today, Lord I am grateful for...

_____

_____

_____

_____

_____

Hear, O Lord, and answer me,
for I am poor and needy. Psalm 86:1

Prayers

_____

_____

_____

_____

_____

_____

_____

_____

_____

_____

_____

_____

_____

_____

_____

Answered Prayers

_____

_____

_____

Sing to him, sing praises to him!
Tell of all his marvelous works.
Psalm 105:2

Lord, today I will praise you for...

_____

_____

_____

_____

You have set our iniquities before you,
our secret sins in the light of your presence. Psalm 90:8

Lord, I confess...

_____

_____

_____

_____

Oh give thanks to the God of heaven;
for his loving kindness endures forever. Psalm 136:26

Today, Lord I am grateful for...

_____

_____

_____

_____

_____

_____

But to you, Yahweh, I have cried.
In the morning, my prayer comes before you.
Psalm 88:13

Prayers
_____

_____

_____

_____

_____

_____

_____

_____

_____

_____

_____

_____

_____

_____

Answered Prayers
_____

_____

_____

_____

Praise the Lord! Give thanks to the Lord,
for he is good, for his loving kindness endures forever.
Psalm 106:1

Lord, today I will praise you for...

_____

_____

_____

_____

Hide your face from my sins,
and blot out all of my iniquities. Psalm 51:9

Lord, I confess...

_____

_____

_____

_____

Let's come before his presence with thanksgiving.
Let's extol him with songs! Psalm 95:2

Today, Lord I am grateful for...

_____

_____

_____

_____

_____

Hear my prayer, O Lord!
Let my cry come to you. Psalm 102:1

Prayers

_____

_____

_____

_____

_____

_____

_____

_____

_____

_____

_____

_____

_____

_____

_____

Answered Prayers

_____

_____

_____

From the rising of the sun to its going down,
the Lord's name is to be praised. Psalm 113:3

Lord, today I will praise you for...

_____

_____

_____

_____

Deliver us, and forgive our sins, for your name's sake.
Psalm 79:9b

Lord, I confess...

_____

_____

_____

_____

Let them offer the sacrifices of thanksgiving,
and declare his deeds with singing Psalm 107:22

Today, Lord I am grateful for...

_____

_____

_____

_____

_____

Lord, hear my voice. Let your ears be attentive to the voice of my petitions. Psalm 130:2

Prayers

_____
_____
_____
_____
_____
_____
_____
_____
_____
_____
_____
_____
_____
_____
_____
_____

Answered Prayers

_____
_____
_____

Date _____

*But we will bless the Lord,
from this time forward and forever more.
Praise the Lord! Psalm 115:18*

Lord, today I will praise you for...

_____

_____

_____

_____

*Sins overwhelmed me,
but you atoned for our transgressions. Psalms 65:3*

Lord, I confess...

_____

_____

_____

_____

*I will give thanks to you, Lord, among the peoples.
I will sing praises to you among the nations. Psalm 57:9*

Today, Lord I am grateful for...

_____

_____

_____

_____

_____

_____

Hear my prayer, O Lord, and give ear to my cry.
Don't be silent at my tears. Psalm 39:12a

Prayers

_____

_____

_____

_____

_____

_____

_____

_____

_____

_____

_____

_____

_____

_____

_____

_____

Answered Prayers

_____

_____

_____

_____

*Let my lips utter praise,
for you teach me your statutes. Psalm 119:171*

Lord, today I will praise you for...

_____

_____

_____

_____

*Wash me thoroughly from my iniquity.
Cleanse me from my sin. Psalm 51:2*

Lord, I confess...

_____

_____

_____

_____

*Praise the Lord! Give thanks to the Lord, for he is good,
for his loving kindness endures forever. Psalm 106:1*

Today, Lord I am grateful for...

_____

_____

_____

_____

_____

_____

Listen to my prayer, God.
Don't hide yourself from my supplication. Psalm 55:1

Prayers

_____

_____

_____

_____

_____

_____

_____

_____

_____

_____

_____

_____

_____

_____

_____

Answered Prayers

_____

_____

_____

I will exalt you, my God, the King.
I will praise your name forever and ever.
Psalm 145:1

Lord, today I will praise you for...

_____

_____

_____

_____

Create in me a clean heart, O God.
Renew a right spirit within me. Psalm 51:10

Lord, I confess...

_____

_____

_____

_____

Give thanks to the Lord! Call on his name!
Make his doings known among the peoples. Psalm 105:1

Today, Lord I am grateful for...

_____

_____

_____

_____

_____

_____

Blessed be God, who has not turned away my prayer,
nor his loving kindness from me. Psalm 66:20

Prayers
_____

_____

_____

_____

_____

_____

_____

_____

_____

_____

_____

_____

_____

_____

_____

Answered Prayers
_____

_____

_____

_____

Every day I will praise you.
I will extol your name forever and ever. Psalm 145:2

Lord, today I will praise you for...

_____

_____

_____

_____

Deliver us, and forgive our sins, for your name's sake.
Psalm 79:9b

Lord, I confess...

_____

_____

_____

_____

Enter into his gates with thanksgiving, and into his courts with
praise. Give thanks to him, and bless his name. Psalm 100:4

Today, Lord I am grateful for...

_____

_____

_____

_____

_____

_____

Hear my prayer, O Lord. Listen to my petitions.
In your faithfulness and righteousness, relieve me.
Psalm 143:1

Prayers
_____
_____
_____
_____
_____
_____
_____
_____
_____
_____
_____
_____
_____
_____
_____
_____

Answered Prayers
_____
_____
_____
_____

While I live, I will praise the Lord.
I will sing praises to my God as long as I exist.
Psalm 146:2

Lord, today I will praise you for...

_____

_____

_____

O Lord, have mercy on me! Heal me,
for I have sinned against you." Psalm 41:4

Lord, I confess...

_____

_____

_____

Sing praise to the Lord, you saints of his.
Give thanks to his holy name. Psalm 30:4

Today, Lord I am grateful for...

_____

_____

_____

_____

_____

Hear my prayer, O God.
Listen to the words of my mouth.
Psalm 54:2

Prayers

_____

_____

_____

_____

_____

_____

_____

_____

_____

_____

_____

_____

_____

_____

_____

_____

Answered Prayers

_____

_____

_____

_____

Praise the Lord, for it is good to sing praises to our God;
for it is pleasant and fitting to praise him. Psalm 147:1

Lord, today I will praise you for...

_____

_____

_____

_____

God, you know my foolishness.
My sins aren't hidden from you. Psalm 69:5

Lord, I confess...

_____

_____

_____

_____

Give thanks to the Lord, for he is good,
for his loving kindness endures forever. Psalm 118:1

Today, Lord I am grateful for...

_____

_____

_____

_____

_____

_____

Hear the voice of my petitions, when I cry to you, when I lift up my hands toward your Most Holy Place. Psalm 28:2

Prayers
_____
_____
_____
_____
_____
_____
_____
_____
_____
_____
_____
_____
_____
_____
_____

Answered Prayers
_____
_____
_____
_____

Let everything that has breath praise the Lord!
Praise the Lord!
Psalm 150:6

Lord, today I will praise you for...

_____

_____

_____

_____

Consider my affliction and my travail.
Forgive all my sins. Psalm 25:18

Lord, I confess...

_____

_____

_____

_____

You are my God, and I will give thanks to you.
You are my God, I will exalt you. Psalm 118:28

Today, Lord I am grateful for...

_____

_____

_____

_____

_____

_____

Let my prayer enter into your presence.
Turn your ear to my cry.
Psalm 88:2

Prayers

_____
_____
_____
_____
_____
_____
_____
_____
_____
_____
_____
_____
_____
_____

Answered Prayers

_____
_____
_____
_____

O come, let us sing unto the Lord
Let us make a joyful noise to the rock of our salvation.
Psalm 95:1

Lord, today I will praise you for...

_____

_____

_____

_____

O Lord, have mercy on me! Heal me,
for I have sinned against you." Psalm 41:4

Lord, I confess...

_____

_____

_____

_____

Oh give thanks to the God of heaven;
for his loving kindness endures forever. Psalm 136:26

Today, Lord I am grateful for...

_____

_____

_____

_____

_____

_____

Hear, O Lord, my righteous plea.
Give ear to my prayer that doesn't go out of deceitful lips.
Psalm 17:1

Prayers

_____

_____

_____

_____

_____

_____

_____

_____

_____

_____

_____

_____

_____

_____

_____

_____

Answered Prayers

_____

_____

_____

My mouth will speak the praise of the Lord.
Let all flesh bless his holy name forever and ever.
Psalm 145:21

Lord, today I will praise you for...

_____

_____

_____

_____

Hide your face from my sins,
and blot out all of my iniquities. Psalm 51:9

Lord, I confess...

_____

_____

_____

_____

I will praise the name of God with a song,
and will magnify him with thanksgiving. Psalm 69:30

Today, Lord I am grateful for...

_____

_____

_____

_____

_____

But to you, Yahweh, I have cried.
In the morning, my prayer comes before you.
Psalm 88:13

Prayers

Answered Prayers

I will be glad and rejoice in you.
I will sing praise to your name, O Most High.
Psalm 9:2

Lord, today I will praise you for...

_____

_____

_____

_____

Consider my affliction and my travail.
Forgive all my sins. Psalm 25:18

Lord, I confess...

_____

_____

_____

_____

For his loving kindness is great toward us.
The Lord's faithfulness endures forever. Psalm 117:2

Today, Lord I am grateful for...

_____

_____

_____

_____

_____

_____

What profit is there in my destruction,
if I go down to the pit? Shall the dust praise you?
Shall it declare your truth? Psalm 30:9

Prayers

_____

_____

_____

_____

_____

_____

_____

_____

_____

_____

_____

_____

_____

_____

_____

Answered Prayers

_____

_____

_____

_____

*My tongue shall talk about your righteousness
and about your praise all day long. Psalm 35:28*

Lord, today I will praise you for...

_____

_____

_____

_____

*Deliver us, and forgive our sins,
for your name's sake. Psalm 79:9*

Lord, I confess...

_____

_____

_____

_____

*I will praise the name of God with a song,
and will magnify him with thanksgiving. Psalm 69:30*

Today, Lord I am grateful for...

_____

_____

_____

_____

_____

_____

Hear my prayer, O Lord!
Let my cry come to you. Psalm 102:1

Prayers

_____

_____

_____

_____

_____

_____

_____

_____

_____

_____

_____

_____

_____

_____

Answered Prayers

_____

_____

_____

_____

Date _____

Sing praises to God! Sing praises!
Sing praises to our King! Sing praises!
Psalm 47:6

Lord, today I will praise you for...

_____
_____
_____
_____

O Lord, have mercy on me! Heal me,
for I have sinned against you." Psalm 41:4

Lord, I confess...

_____
_____
_____
_____

So we, your people and sheep of your pasture, will give you thanks
forever. We will praise you forever, to all generations.
Psalm 79:13

Today, Lord I am grateful for...

_____
_____
_____
_____
_____
_____

Hear the voice of my petitions,
when I cry to you, when I lift up my hands
toward your Most Holy Place. Psalm 28:2

Prayers

_____
_____
_____
_____
_____
_____
_____
_____
_____
_____
_____
_____
_____
_____

Answered Prayers

_____
_____
_____

Lord, open my lips.
My mouth will declare your praise.
Psalm 51:15

Lord, today I will praise you for... _____

_____

_____

_____

_____

Deliver us, and forgive our sins, for your name's sake.
Psalm 79:9b

Lord, I confess... _____

_____

_____

_____

_____

Let's come before his presence with thanksgiving.
Let's extol him with songs! Psalm 95:2

Today, Lord I am grateful for... _____

_____

_____

_____

_____

_____

_____

Hear, O Lord, my prayer.
Listen to the voice of my petitions.
Psalm 86:6

Prayers

_____

_____

_____

_____

_____

_____

_____

_____

_____

_____

_____

_____

_____

_____

_____

_____

Answered Prayers

_____

_____

_____

_____

My heart is steadfast, God. My heart is steadfast.
I will sing, yes, I will sing praises.
Psalm 57:7

Lord, today I will praise you for...

_____

_____

_____

_____

Sins overwhelmed me,
but you atoned for our transgressions. Psalms 65:3

Lord, I confess...

_____

_____

_____

_____

Let them offer the sacrifices of thanksgiving,
and declare his deeds with singing Psalm 107:22

Today, Lord I am grateful for...

_____

_____

_____

_____

_____

_____

Lord, hear my voice. Let your ears be attentive to the voice of my petitions. Psalm 130:2

Prayers

_____

_____

_____

_____

_____

_____

_____

_____

_____

_____

_____

_____

_____

Answered Prayers

_____

_____

_____

*Praise be to the Lord God,
the God of Israel, who alone does marvelous deeds.
Psalm 72:18*

Lord, today I will praise you for...

_____

_____

_____

_____

*Create in me a clean heart, O God.
Renew a right spirit within me. Psalm 51:10*

Lord, I confess...

_____

_____

_____

_____

*I will give thanks to the Lord
according to his righteousness, Psalm 7:17*

Today, Lord I am grateful for...

_____

_____

_____

_____

_____

_____

Hear my prayer, O Lord. Listen to my petitions.
In your faithfulness and righteousness, relieve me.
Psalm 143:1

Prayers

_____

_____

_____

_____

_____

_____

_____

_____

_____

_____

_____

_____

_____

_____

_____

_____

Answered Prayers

_____

_____

_____

_____

To you, my strength, I will sing praises.
For God is my high tower, the God of my mercy.
Psalm 59:17

Lord, today I will praise you for...

_____

_____

_____

_____

Wash me thoroughly from my iniquity.
Cleanse me from my sin. Psalm 51:2

Lord, I confess...

_____

_____

_____

_____

Sing praise to the Lord, you saints of his.
Give thanks to his holy name. Psalm 30:4

Today, Lord I am grateful for...

_____

_____

_____

_____

_____

_____

Let my soul live, that I may praise you.
Let your ordinances help me. Psalm 119:175

Prayers
_____
_____
_____
_____
_____
_____
_____
_____
_____
_____
_____
_____
_____
_____

Answered Prayers
_____
_____
_____
_____

Date _____

*Because your loving kindness is better than life,
my lips shall praise you Psalm 63:3*

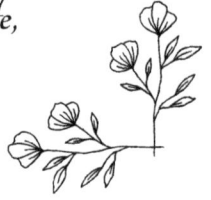

Lord, today I will praise you for...

_____
_____
_____
_____

*Hide your face from my sins,
and blot out all of my iniquities. Psalm 51:9*

Lord, I confess...

_____
_____
_____
_____

*I will give thanks to you, Lord, among the peoples.
I will sing praises to you among the nations. Psalm 57:9*

Today, Lord I am grateful for...

_____
_____
_____
_____
_____
_____

Listen to my prayer, God.
Don't hide yourself from my supplication.
Psalm 55:1

Prayers

_____

_____

_____

_____

_____

_____

_____

_____

_____

_____

_____

_____

_____

_____

_____

Answered Prayers

_____

_____

_____

_____

Let the peoples praise you, God.
Let all the peoples praise you. Psalm 67:5

Lord, today I will praise you for...

_____

_____

_____

_____

You have set our iniquities before you,
our secret sins in the light of your presence. Psalm 90:8

Lord, I confess...

_____

_____

_____

_____

We give thanks to you, God. We give thanks,
for your Name is near. Psalm 75:1a

Today, Lord I am grateful for...

_____

_____

_____

_____

_____

_____

Answer me when I call, God of my righteousness.
Give me relief from my distress. Have mercy on me,
and hear my prayer. Psalm 4:1

Prayers
_____

_____

_____

_____

_____

_____

_____

_____

_____

_____

_____

_____

_____

_____

_____

Answered Prayers
_____

_____

_____

_____

I will praise the name of God with a song,
and will magnify him with thanksgiving.
Psalm 69:30

Lord, today I will praise you for... _____

_____

_____

_____

Deliver us, and forgive our sins, for your name's sake.
Psalm 79:96

Lord, I confess... _____

_____

_____

_____

Sing praise to Yahweh, you saints of his.
Give thanks to his holy name. Psalm 30:4

Today, Lord I am grateful for... _____

_____

_____

_____

_____

_____

Let my soul live, that I may praise you.
Let your ordinances help me. Psalm 119:175

Prayers

_____

_____

_____

_____

_____

_____

_____

_____

_____

_____

_____

_____

_____

Answered Prayers

_____

_____

_____

Praise the Lord!

Give thanks to the Lord,
for He is good,
For his loving kindness
endures forever.

Psalm 106:1

*From the rising of the sun to its going down,
the Lord's name is to be praised. Psalm 113:3*

Lord, today I will praise you for...

_____

_____

_____

_____

*Deliver us, and forgive our sins, for your name's sake.
Psalm 79:9b*

Lord, I confess...

_____

_____

_____

_____

*Let them offer the sacrifices of thanksgiving,
and declare his deeds with singing Psalm 107:22*

Today, Lord I am grateful for...

_____

_____

_____

_____

_____

_____

Lord, hear my voice. Let your ears be attentive to the voice of my petitions. Psalm 130:2

Prayers

_____

_____

_____

_____

_____

_____

_____

_____

_____

_____

_____

_____

_____

Answered Prayers

_____

_____

_____

But we will bless the Lord,
from this time forward and forever more.
Praise the Lord! Psalm 115:18

Lord, today I will praise you for...

_____

_____

_____

_____

Sins overwhelmed me,
but you atoned for our transgressions. Psalms 65:3

Lord, I confess...

_____

_____

_____

_____

I will give thanks to you, Lord, among the peoples.
I will sing praises to you among the nations. Psalm 57:9

Today, Lord I am grateful for...

_____

_____

_____

_____

_____

_____

Hear my prayer, O Lord, and give ear to my cry.
Don't be silent at my tears. Psalm 39:12a

Prayers

_____

_____

_____

_____

_____

_____

_____

_____

_____

_____

_____

_____

_____

_____

_____

Answered Prayers

_____

_____

_____

Let my lips utter praise,
for you teach me your statutes. Psalm 119:171

Lord, today I will praise you for...

_____

_____

_____

_____

Wash me thoroughly from my iniquity.
Cleanse me from my sin. Psalm 51:2

Lord, I confess...

_____

_____

_____

_____

Praise the Lord! Give thanks to the Lord, for he is good,
for his loving kindness endures forever. Psalm 106:1

Today, Lord I am grateful for...

_____

_____

_____

_____

_____

_____

Listen to my prayer, God.
Don't hide yourself from my supplication. Psalm 55:1

Prayers

_____

_____

_____

_____

_____

_____

_____

_____

_____

_____

_____

_____

_____

Answered Prayers

_____

_____

_____

I will exalt you, my God, the King.
I will praise your name forever and ever.
Psalm 145:1

Lord, today I will praise you for... _____

_____

_____

_____

Create in me a clean heart, O God.
Renew a right spirit within me. Psalm 51:10

Lord, I confess... _____

_____

_____

_____

Give thanks to the Lord! Call on his name!
Make his doings known among the peoples. Psalm 105:1

Today, Lord I am grateful for... _____

_____

_____

_____

_____

_____

Blessed be God, who has not turned away my prayer, nor his loving kindness from me. Psalm 66:20

Prayers

_____

_____

_____

_____

_____

_____

_____

_____

_____

_____

_____

_____

_____

_____

_____

Answered Prayers

_____

_____

_____

Every day I will praise you.
I will extol your name forever and ever. Psalm 145:2

Lord, today I will praise you for...

_____

_____

_____

_____

Deliver us, and forgive our sins, for your name's sake.
Psalm 79:9b

Lord, I confess...

_____

_____

_____

_____

Enter into his gates with thanksgiving, and into his courts with praise.
Give thanks to him, and bless his name. Psalm 100:4

Today, Lord I am grateful for...

_____

_____

_____

_____

_____

_____

Hear my prayer, O Lord. Listen to my petitions.
In your faithfulness and righteousness, relieve me.
Psalm 143:1

Prayers

_____

_____

_____

_____

_____

_____

_____

_____

_____

_____

_____

_____

_____

_____

Answered Prayers

_____

_____

_____

While I live, I will praise the Lord.
I will sing praises to my God as long as I exist.
Psalm 146:2

Lord, today I will praise you for...

_____

_____

_____

_____

O Lord, have mercy on me! Heal me,
for I have sinned against you." Psalm 41:4

Lord, I confess...

_____

_____

_____

_____

Sing praise to the Lord, you saints of his.
Give thanks to his holy name. Psalm 30:4

Today, Lord I am grateful for...

_____

_____

_____

_____

_____

_____

Hear my prayer, O God.
Listen to the words of my mouth.
Psalm 54:2

Prayers

_____

_____

_____

_____

_____

_____

_____

_____

_____

_____

_____

_____

_____

Answered Prayers

_____

_____

_____

_____

Praise the Lord, for it is good to sing praises to our God;
for it is pleasant and fitting to praise him. Psalm 147:1

Lord, today I will praise you for...

_____

_____

_____

_____

God, you know my foolishness.
My sins aren't hidden from you. Psalm 69:5

Lord, I confess...

_____

_____

_____

_____

Give thanks to the Lord, for he is good,
for his loving kindness endures forever. Psalm 118:1

Today, Lord I am grateful for...

_____

_____

_____

_____

_____

Hear the voice of my petitions, when I cry to you, when I lift up my hands toward your Most Holy Place. Psalm 28:2

Prayers
_____
_____
_____
_____
_____
_____
_____
_____
_____
_____
_____
_____
_____
_____

Answered Prayers
_____
_____
_____
_____

Let everything that has breath praise the Lord!
Praise the Lord!
Psalm 150:6

Lord, today I will praise you for...

_____

_____

_____

_____

Consider my affliction and my travail.
Forgive all my sins. Psalm 25:18

Lord, I confess...

_____

_____

_____

_____

You are my God, and I will give thanks to you.
You are my God, I will exalt you. Psalm 118:28

Today, Lord I am grateful for...

_____

_____

_____

_____

_____

_____

Let my prayer enter into your presence.
Turn your ear to my cry.
Psalm 88:2

Prayers

_____

_____

_____

_____

_____

_____

_____

_____

_____

_____

_____

_____

_____

Answered Prayers

_____

_____

_____

O come, let us sing unto the Lord
Let us make a joyful noise to the rock of our salvation.
Psalm 95:1

Lord, today I will praise you for...

_____

_____

_____

_____

O Lord, have mercy on me! Heal me,
for I have sinned against you." Psalm 41:4

Lord, I confess...

_____

_____

_____

_____

Oh give thanks to the God of heaven;
for his loving kindness endures forever. Psalm 136:26

Today, Lord I am grateful for...

_____

_____

_____

_____

_____

_____

Hear, O Lord, my righteous plea.
Give ear to my prayer that doesn't go out of deceitful lips.
Psalm 17:1

Prayers

_____
_____
_____
_____
_____
_____
_____
_____
_____
_____
_____
_____
_____
_____

Answered Prayers

_____
_____
_____
_____

My mouth will speak the praise of the Lord.
Let all flesh bless his holy name forever and ever.
Psalm 145:21

Lord, today I will praise you for...

_____

_____

_____

_____

Hide your face from my sins,
and blot out all of my iniquities. Psalm 51:9

Lord, I confess...

_____

_____

_____

_____

I will praise the name of God with a song,
and will magnify him with thanksgiving. Psalm 69:30

Today, Lord I am grateful for...

_____

_____

_____

_____

_____

_____

But to you, Yahweh, I have cried.
In the morning, my prayer comes before you.
Psalm 88:13

Prayers
_____
_____
_____
_____
_____
_____
_____
_____
_____
_____
_____
_____
_____
_____

Answered Prayers
_____
_____
_____
_____

I will be glad and rejoice in you.
I will sing praise to your name, O Most High.
Psalm 9:2

Lord, today I will praise you for...

_____

_____

_____

_____

Consider my affliction and my travail.
Forgive all my sins. Psalm 25:18

Lord, I confess...

_____

_____

_____

_____

For his loving kindness is great toward us.
The Lord's faithfulness endures forever. Psalm 117:2

Today, Lord I am grateful for...

_____

_____

_____

_____

_____

What profit is there in my destruction,
if I go down to the pit? Shall the dust praise you?
Shall it declare your truth? Psalm 30:9

Prayers

_____

_____

_____

_____

_____

_____

_____

_____

_____

_____

_____

_____

Answered Prayers

_____

_____

_____

*My tongue shall talk about your righteousness
and about your praise all day long. Psalm 35:28*

Lord, today I will praise you for...

_____

_____

_____

_____

*Deliver us, and forgive our sins,
for your name's sake. Psalm 79:9*

Lord, I confess...

_____

_____

_____

_____

*I will praise the name of God with a song,
and will magnify him with thanksgiving. Psalm 69:30*

Today, Lord I am grateful for...

_____

_____

_____

_____

_____

_____

Hear my prayer, O Lord!
Let my cry come to you. Psalm 102:1

Prayers

_____

_____

_____

_____

_____

_____

_____

_____

_____

_____

_____

_____

_____

_____

Answered Prayers

_____

_____

_____

_____

Date _____

Sing praises to God! Sing praises!
Sing praises to our King! Sing praises!
Psalm 47:6

Lord, today I will praise you for...

_____

_____

_____

_____

O Lord, have mercy on me! Heal me,
for I have sinned against you." Psalm 41:4

Lord, I confess...

_____

_____

_____

_____

So we, your people and sheep of your pasture, will give you thanks
forever. We will praise you forever, to all generations. Psalm 79:13

Today, Lord I am grateful for...

_____

_____

_____

_____

_____

_____

Hear the voice of my petitions,
when I cry to you, when I lift up my hands
toward your Most Holy Place. Psalm 28:2

Prayers

_____

_____

_____

_____

_____

_____

_____

_____

_____

_____

_____

_____

_____

Answered Prayers

_____

_____

_____

_____

Lord, open my lips.
My mouth will declare your praise.
Psalm 51:15

Lord, today I will praise you for...

_____

_____

_____

_____

Deliver us, and forgive our sins, for your name's sake.
Psalm 79:9b

Lord, I confess...

_____

_____

_____

_____

Let's come before his presence with thanksgiving.
Let's extol him with songs! Psalm 95:2

Today, Lord I am grateful for...

_____

_____

_____

_____

_____

_____

Hear, O Lord, my prayer.
Listen to the voice of my petitions.
Psalm 86:6

Prayers

_____

_____

_____

_____

_____

_____

_____

_____

_____

_____

_____

_____

_____

_____

_____

Answered Prayers

_____

_____

_____

_____

My heart is steadfast, God. My heart is steadfast.
I will sing, yes, I will sing praises.
Psalm 57:7

Lord, today I will praise you for...

_____

_____

_____

_____

Sins overwhelmed me,
but you atoned for our transgressions. Psalms 65:3

Lord, I confess...

_____

_____

_____

_____

Let them offer the sacrifices of thanksgiving,
and declare his deeds with singing Psalm 107:22

Today, Lord I am grateful for...

_____

_____

_____

_____

_____

_____

Lord, hear my voice. Let your ears be attentive to the voice of my petitions. Psalm 130:2

Prayers

_____

_____

_____

_____

_____

_____

_____

_____

_____

_____

_____

_____

_____

_____

Answered Prayers

_____

_____

_____

*Praise be to the Lord God,
the God of Israel, who alone does marvelous deeds.
Psalm 72:18*

Lord, today I will praise you for...

_____

_____

_____

_____

*Create in me a clean heart, O God.
Renew a right spirit within me. Psalm 51:10*

Lord, I confess...

_____

_____

_____

_____

*I will give thanks to the Lord
according to his righteousness, Psalm 7:17*

Today, Lord I am grateful for...

_____

_____

_____

_____

_____

_____

Hear my prayer, O Lord. Listen to my petitions.
In your faithfulness and righteousness, relieve me.
Psalm 143:1

Prayers
_____
_____
_____
_____
_____
_____
_____
_____
_____
_____
_____
_____
_____
_____
_____

Answered Prayers
_____
_____
_____

To you, my strength, I will sing praises.
For God is my high tower, the God of my mercy.
Psalm 59:17

Lord, today I will praise you for...

_____

_____

_____

_____

Wash me thoroughly from my iniquity.
Cleanse me from my sin. Psalm 51:2

Lord, I confess...

_____

_____

_____

_____

Sing praise to the Lord, you saints of his.
Give thanks to his holy name. Psalm 30:4

Today, Lord I am grateful for...

_____

_____

_____

_____

_____

_____

Let my soul live, that I may praise you.
Let your ordinances help me. Psalm 119:175

Prayers
_____
_____
_____
_____
_____
_____
_____
_____
_____
_____
_____
_____
_____
_____

Answered Prayers
_____
_____
_____
_____

Date _____

*Because your loving kindness is better than life,
my lips shall praise you Psalm 63:3*

Lord, today I will praise you for...

_____

_____

_____

_____

*Hide your face from my sins,
and blot out all of my iniquities. Psalm 51:9*

Lord, I confess...

_____

_____

_____

_____

*I will give thanks to you, Lord, among the peoples.
I will sing praises to you among the nations. Psalm 57:9*

Today, Lord I am grateful for...

_____

_____

_____

_____

_____

Listen to my prayer, God.
Don't hide yourself from my supplication.
Psalm 55:1

Prayers

_____

_____

_____

_____

_____

_____

_____

_____

_____

_____

_____

_____

_____

_____

Answered Prayers

_____

_____

_____

Let the peoples praise you, God.
Let all the peoples praise you. Psalm 67:5

Lord, today I will praise you for...

_____

_____

_____

_____

You have set our iniquities before you,
our secret sins in the light of your presence. Psalm 90:8

Lord, I confess...

_____

_____

_____

_____

We give thanks to you, God. We give thanks,
for your Name is near. Psalm 75:1a

Today, Lord I am grateful for...

_____

_____

_____

_____

_____

Answer me when I call, God of my righteousness.
Give me relief from my distress. Have mercy on me,
and hear my prayer. Psalm 4:1

Prayers

_____

_____

_____

_____

_____

_____

_____

_____

_____

_____

_____

_____

Answered Prayers

_____

_____

_____

*I will praise the name of God with a song,
and will magnify him with thanksgiving.
Psalm 69:30*

Lord, today I will praise you for... _____

_____

_____

_____

_____

*Deliver us, and forgive our sins, for your name's sake.
Psalm 79:9b*

Lord, I confess... _____

_____

_____

_____

_____

*Sing praise to Yahweh, you saints of his.
Give thanks to his holy name. Psalm 30:4*

Today, Lord I am grateful for... _____

_____

_____

_____

_____

_____

Let my soul live, that I may praise you.
Let your ordinances help me. Psalm 119:175

Prayers

_____

_____

_____

_____

_____

_____

_____

_____

_____

_____

_____

_____

_____

_____

Answered Prayers

_____

_____

_____

My lips shall shout for joy!
My soul, which you have redeemed, sings praises to you!
Psalm 71:23

Lord, today I will praise you for...

_____

_____

_____

_____

O Lord, have mercy on me! Heal me,
for I have sinned against you." Psalm 41:4

Lord, I confess...

_____

_____

_____

_____

I will give thanks to you, Lord, among the peoples.
I will sing praises to you among the nations. Psalm 57:9

Today, Lord I am grateful for...

_____

_____

_____

_____

_____

_____

Hear my prayer, O Lord, and give ear to my cry.
Don't be silent at my tears. Psalm 39:12a

Prayers
_____
_____
_____
_____
_____
_____
_____
_____
_____
_____
_____
_____
_____
_____

Answered Prayers
_____
_____
_____
_____

I will praise you, Lord my God, with my whole heart.
I will glorify your name forever more. Psalm 86:12

Lord, today I will praise you for...

_____

_____

_____

_____

God, you know my foolishness.
My sins aren't hidden from you. Psalm 69:5

Lord, I confess...

_____

_____

_____

_____

We give thanks to you, God. We give thanks, for your
Name is near. Men tell about your wondrous works.
Psalm 75:1

Today, Lord I am grateful for...

_____

_____

_____

_____

_____

_____

Listen to my prayer, God.
Don't hide yourself from my supplication. Psalm 55:1

Prayers

_____

_____

_____

_____

_____

_____

_____

_____

_____

_____

_____

_____

_____

_____

_____

Answered Prayers

_____

_____

_____

Date _____

Make a joyful noise to the Lord, all the earth!
Burst out and sing for joy, yes, sing praises!
Psalm 98:4

Lord, today I will praise you for...

_____
_____
_____
_____

You have set our iniquities before you,
our secret sins in the light of your presence. Psalm 90:8

Lord, I confess...

_____
_____
_____
_____

Give thanks to the Lord! Call on his name!
Make his doings known among the peoples. Psalm 105:1

Today, Lord I am grateful for...

_____
_____
_____
_____
_____
_____

Answer me when I call, God of my righteousness.
Give me relief from my distress. Have mercy on me,
and hear my prayer. Psalm 4:1

Prayers

_____

_____

_____

_____

_____

_____

_____

_____

_____

_____

_____

_____

_____

_____

_____

_____

Answered Prayers

_____

_____

_____

For the Lord is great, and greatly to be praised!
He is to be feared above all gods. Psalm 96:4

Lord, today I will praise you for...

_____

_____

_____

_____

Hide your face from my sins,
and blot out all of my iniquities. Psalm 51:9

Lord, I confess...

_____

_____

_____

_____

Praise the Lord! Give thanks to the Lord, for he is good,
for his loving kindness endures forever. Psalm 106:1

Today, Lord I am grateful for...

_____

_____

_____

_____

_____

_____

Hear, O Lord, my righteous plea.
Give ear to my prayer that doesn't go out of deceitful lips.
Psalm 17:1

Prayers

_____

_____

_____

_____

_____

_____

_____

_____

_____

_____

_____

_____

_____

Answered Prayers

_____

_____

_____

I will sing of loving kindness and justice.
To you, O Lord, I will sing praises. Psalm 101:1

Lord, today I will praise you for...

_____

_____

_____

_____

Wash me thoroughly from my iniquity.
Cleanse me from my sin. Psalm 51:2

Lord, I confess...

_____

_____

_____

_____

I will give great thanks to the Lord with my mouth.
Yes, I will praise him among the multitude. Psalm 109:30

Today, Lord I am grateful for...

_____

_____

_____

_____

_____

_____

Hear my prayer, God.
Listen to the words of my mouth. Psalm 54:2

Prayers

_____

_____

_____

_____

_____

_____

_____

_____

_____

_____

_____

_____

_____

Answered Prayers

_____

_____

_____

Praise the Lord, my soul!
All that is within me, praise his holy name!
Psalm 103:1

Lord, today I will praise you for...

_____

_____

_____

_____

Create in me a clean heart, O God.
Renew a right spirit within me. Psalm 51:10

Lord, I confess...

_____

_____

_____

_____

Give thanks to the Lord, for he is good,
for his loving kindness endures forever. Psalm 118:1

Today, Lord I am grateful for...

_____

_____

_____

_____

_____

_____

Blessed be God, who has not turned away my prayer, nor his loving kindness from me. Psalm 66:20

Prayers

_____

_____

_____

_____

_____

_____

_____

_____

_____

_____

_____

_____

_____

Answered Prayers

_____

_____

_____

Praise the Lord, my soul,
and don't forget all his benefits. Psalm 103:2

Lord, today I will praise you for...

_____

_____

_____

_____

Sins overwhelmed me,
but you atoned for our transgressions. Psalms 65:3

Lord, I confess...

_____

_____

_____

_____

I will give thanks to you, for you have answered me,
and have become my salvation. Psalm 118:21

Today, Lord I am grateful for...

_____

_____

_____

_____

_____

_____

Let my prayer enter into your presence.
Turn your ear to my cry. Psalm 88:2

Prayers

_____

_____

_____

_____

_____

_____

_____

_____

_____

_____

_____

_____

_____

_____

_____

Answered Prayers

_____

_____

_____

Date _____

I will sing to the Lord as long as I live.
I will sing praise to my God while I have any being.
Psalm 104:33

Lord, today I will praise you for...

_____
_____
_____
_____

Consider my affliction and my travail.
Forgive all my sins. Psalm 25:18

Lord, I confess...

_____
_____
_____
_____

You are my God, and I will give thanks to you.
You are my God, I will exalt you. Psalm 118:28

Today, Lord I am grateful for...

_____
_____
_____
_____
_____

Hear, O Lord, and answer me,
for I am poor and needy. Psalm 86:1

Prayers

_____

_____

_____

_____

_____

_____

_____

_____

_____

_____

_____

_____

_____

_____

_____

Answered Prayers

_____

_____

_____

_____

Sing to him, sing praises to him!
Tell of all his marvelous works.
Psalm 105:2

Lord, today I will praise you for...

_____

_____

_____

_____

You have set our iniquities before you,
our secret sins in the light of your presence. Psalm 90:8

Lord, I confess...

_____

_____

_____

_____

Oh give thanks to the God of heaven;
for his loving kindness endures forever. Psalm 136:26

Today, Lord I am grateful for...

_____

_____

_____

_____

_____

_____

But to you, Yahweh, I have cried.
In the morning, my prayer comes before you.
Psalm 88:13

Prayers

_____

_____

_____

_____

_____

_____

_____

_____

_____

_____

_____

_____

_____

Answered Prayers

_____

_____

_____

_____

Praise the Lord! Give thanks to the Lord,
for he is good, for his loving kindness endures forever.
Psalm 106:1

Lord, today I will praise you for...

_____

_____

_____

_____

Hide your face from my sins,
and blot out all of my iniquities. Psalm 51:9

Lord, I confess...

_____

_____

_____

_____

Let's come before his presence with thanksgiving.
Let's extol him with songs! Psalm 95:2

Today, Lord I am grateful for...

_____

_____

_____

_____

_____

_____

Hear my prayer, O Lord!
Let my cry come to you. Psalm 102:1

Prayers

_____

_____

_____

_____

_____

_____

_____

_____

_____

_____

_____

_____

_____

Answered Prayers

_____

_____

_____

You are my God,
and I will give thanks to you.
You are my God,
I will exalt you.

Psalm 118:28

Lightning Source UK Ltd.
Milton Keynes UK
UKHW010924190921
390665UK00007B/170